Let's Make a
Bar Graph

by Robin Nelson

Lerner Publications Company · Minneapolis

Nan has a cat.

Nan wants to ask her
classmates about their pets.

Nan asks what pets her classmates have. She **surveys** her class.

The answers are her **data**.

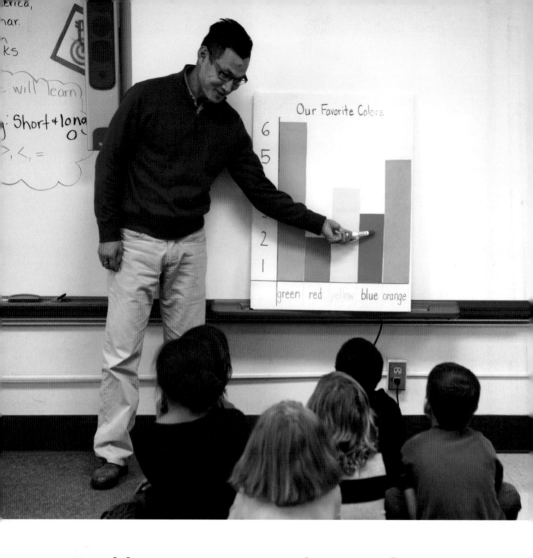

Nan can make a **bar graph** with her data.

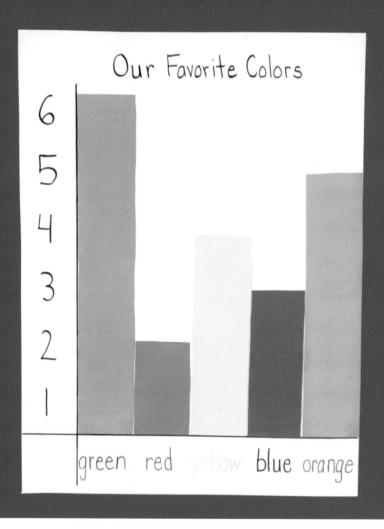

A bar graph shows data using **bars**.

cat　　dog　　fish　　bird

kinds of pets

Nan lists the kinds of pets on the bottom of her bar graph.

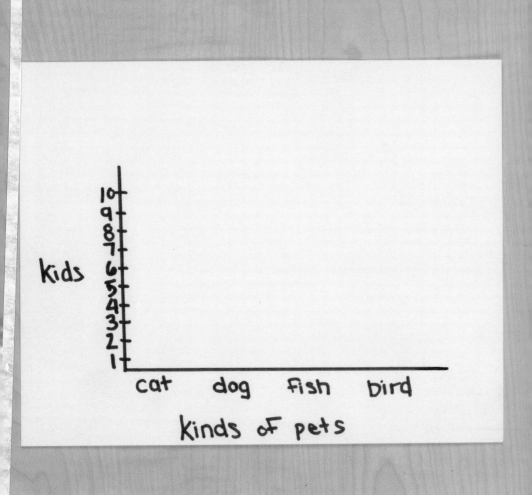

She writes numbers on the
side of her bar graph.

Nan draws a bar for each
kind of pet. Each bar will

have a different color.

Four kids have cats.

Nan draws a yellow bar
over the word *cat*.

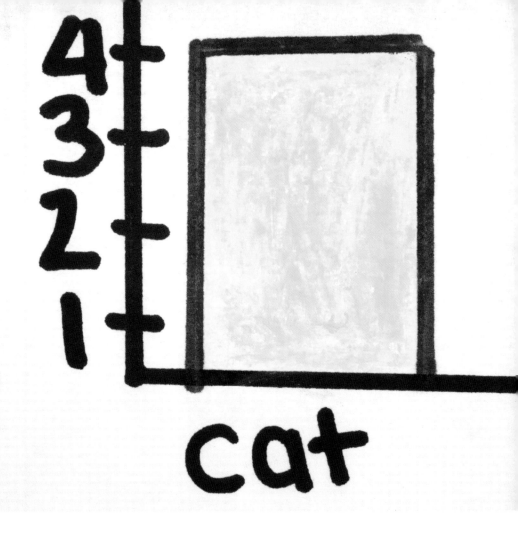

The bar goes up to the number four.

Nan colors the bars for the other kinds of pets.

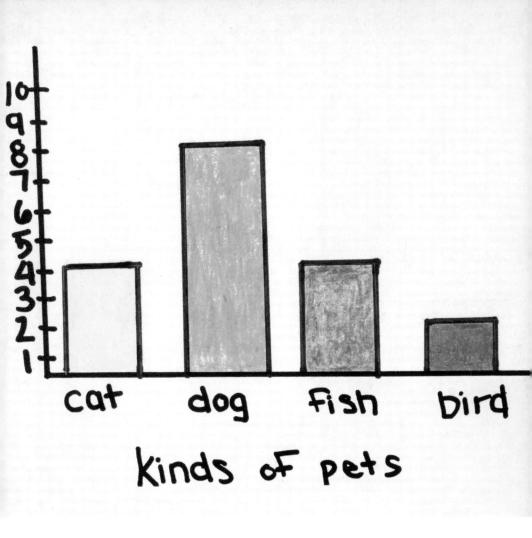

She uses her data to know
how tall to make each bar.

Nan adds a title to her bar graph.

She shares her bar graph
with her class.

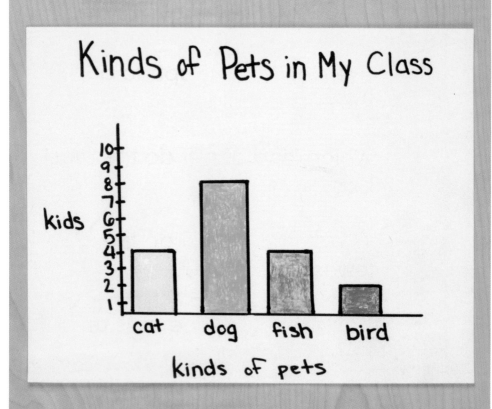

Kinds of Pets in My Class

Use Nan's bar graph to answer these questions.

Which kind of pet do the most kids have?

Which kind of pet do the fewest kids have?

Do more kids have cats or dogs?

How many more kids have dogs than birds?

How to Make a Bar Graph

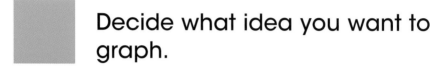

Decide what idea you want to graph.

Ask questions to get data.

Label the bottom and side of your graph.

Use your data to draw your bars. Give each bar a different color

Add a title.

Glossary

 bar graph – a graph that uses bars to show information

 bars – shapes that are long and not wide

 data – information used to create a graph

 label – to write words on a graph that tell about the data

 surveys – asks a question to gather information

Index

All images in this book are used with the permission of: © Todd Strand/Independent Picture Service except: © Erica Johnson/Independent Picture Service, p. 2.

Front cover: © Jon Fischer/Independent Picture Service.

Main body text set in ITC Avant Garde Gothic Std Medium 21/25.
Typeface provided by Adobe Systems

Lerner Publications Company
A division of Lerner Publishing Group, Inc.
241 First Avenue North
Minneapolis, MN 55401 U.S.A.

Website address: www.lernerbooks.com

Library of Congress Cataloging-in-Publication Data

Nelson, Robin, 1971–
    Let's make a bar graph / by Robin Nelson.
        p.   cm. — (First step nonfiction—graph it!)
    Includes index.
    ISBN 978–0–7613–8972–9 (lib. bdg. : alk. paper)
    1. Mathematics—Graphic methods—Juvenile literature. I. Title.
QA40.5.N45 2013
001.4'226—dc23   2011044696

Manufactured in the United States of America
1 – BC – 7/15/12